# GUINEA PIG B
*The 56 year experiment*

R. Buckminster Fuller

Critical Path Publishing, California

For information, address
**Critical Path Publishing**
**PO Box 1073, Clayton, CA 94517**
**Email: info@criticalpathpublishing.org     Phone: 925.672.4464**
**www.criticalpathpublishing.org**

Reprinted with the permission of the Estate of R. Buckminster Fuller. Guinea Pig B was first published as the introduction to the book, *Inventions, The Patented Works of R. Buckminster Fuller*, St. Martins Press, 1983, ISBN 0-312-43477-4. It was also published in *Buckminster Fuller, Anthology for the New Millennium*, St. Martins Press, 2001, ISBN 0-312-26639-1.

For more information on Fuller's life and work please contact:
The Buckminster Fuller Institute
181 N 11th St, Suite 402
Brooklyn, NY 11211
Phone: 718.290.9280
Or see their comprehensive web site: www.bfi.org

Critical Path Publishing Edition
First Printing, April 2003
Second Printing, February 2004
Third Printing, March 2008
ISBN 0-9740605-0-X
Library of Congress Control Number: 2003105014

Cover and book design by
    Cause Change, Design & Creative: info@causechange.com
Cover and inside photos by
    Wernher Krutein: www.photovault.com
Printing by Secord Printing: www.secordprinting.com

Printed on recycled paper

# APPRECIATION

One of the main reasons Critical Path Publishing (CPP) exists is to get R. Buckminster Fuller material into the hands of as many people as possible. Reprinting books by him is one way to accomplish this. CPP feels that the experiment that Bucky (as he was affectionately known) committed his life to resulted in discoveries and perspectives that are exactly what humanity needs in order to live on "Spaceship Earth" together in optimal harmony, balance, and prosperity. Bucky felt humanity is positioned to "carry on in a far more intelligent way than ever before." Having his work widely accessible is an important part of actualizing his realization that humanity is designed for, and has the option to be, an incredible success. We all can play a role in this scenario and Bucky's ideas/teaching/results are a wonderful example of the possibilities.

Guinea Pig B could not have been published without the help and services of may people who are very special to CPP: To Jaime Snyder and John Ferry of the R. Buckminster Fuller Estate for encouragement, permission, support, and guidance; to Allegra Fuller Snyder for a wonderful introduction; to Bob Schildgen for quality editing of non-Bucky material; to Werhner Krutein for exquisite photos; to Keri Secord of Secord Printing for printing and delivering this book with extremely thoughtful, efficient, and exemplary service; to CPP shareholders for their continuing support, and an extra special appreciation to A.J. Ross, a masterful designer, who designed the fabulous cover and the book's layout while paying close attention to all of the details that resulted in this inspiring addition to the extraordinary legacy of R. Buckminster Fuller. Thank you all for sharing our vision and for your unselfish and synergetic contributions.

With humble and unbounded appreciation,

Critical Path Publishing

# INTRODUCTION

I think my father was very honest in his appraisal of himself. He said he felt he was just an average human being. I think he was a very average man who developed a strategy to take full advantage of his capabilities, capabilities that are inherent in all of us. I think it is important to recognize that it took him about thirty-two years to sort out his priorities and for him to understand himself well enough to really pursue the course of action that he then pursued. It was a course of action that demanded his full integrity in listening to himself, in challenging himself, and at the same time being deeply aware of all that surrounded him.

Yes, I think he was an average man, but he developed certain qualities within himself that changed the ordinary into more than ordinary. First, I think, is discipline: self-discipline. He was very demanding of himself and had exquisite ability to respond to these demands. On my mother and father's 25th wedding anniversary, as a gift to my mother, he decided he would stop smoking and drinking. My father, as was very typical of a young man growing up in his time, had been an enthusiastic social drinker and he was a good pack-a-day cigarette smoker. On that very day, he stopped both smoking and drinking, for the rest of his life. This, to me, was an "extra" ordinary example of his self-discipline. About ten years later he had gained quite a lot of weight. So he put himself on a high protein diet, which he remained on almost until the end of his life. He lost some forty or fifty pounds. These are things that each of us can do. It just takes the challenge that my father was willing to pose to himself.

His thinking was as disciplined. He was meticulous in challenging his own thoughts and ideas, making sure that he was thinking clearly, that he was not relying on someone else's hearsay but basing his own thoughts and ideas on his own experience. When he read anything he always had a dictionary close at hand because he never let himself look at a word, that he didn't fully understand, and pass it by. He must understand not only its meaning but also its root. He would then be very disciplined in using that word correctly; using it in the way he felt was inherent in the word itself. This discipline, in later years, resulted in his making new words for himself when he found no term that adequately expressed his thought. This sometimes makes a first reading of some of his work challenging for others because they also need a Buckminster Fuller dictionary close at hand in order to understand what he was really getting at. Incidentally such a series of volumes does exist, though not readily available. It is the wonderful Synergetics Dictionary, which was edited by E. J. Applewhite.

He also arrived at the decision to make sense–not money, and never take a job just to earn money. He made that decision with responsibility as well as discipline. This sense of responsibility grew to encompass a sense of one man's responsibility to all of humanity. His root of responsibility was a sense that his actions always had repercussions and reactions on others. He must always make decisions that were fully predicated on a sense of equal responsibility to himself, to his family, and to the world.

His course of action for himself and for others was not easy. I think my mother, his wife of sixty-seven years, played an extraordinary role in making his course of action possible. She was a very strong person, full of very quiet dignity. She was completely supportive of my father's decisions and lifestyle because, I think, she was very clear about herself and who she was. There was a sense of strength that he received from her. She was always there, in no way a "yes" person, but nevertheless completely supportive.

And what were they like as parents? They taught me to grow up to be myself. That is the essence of what we all should be, but to also understand that really being yourself required self discipline and responsibility. They allowed something to emerge in me that was both uniquely me and yet at the same time average because I was simply being what I was capable of being – what we are all capable of being. I think that is what this little book is about. And it is a very exciting idea because it is powerful in its simplicity.

*~Allegra Fuller Snyder*
*April 2003*

# GUINEA PIG B

I AM NOW CLOSE TO 88 and I am confident that the only thing important about me is that I am an average healthy human. I am also a living case history of a thoroughly documented, half-century, search-and-research project designed to discover what, if anything, an unknown, moneyless individual, with a dependent wife and newborn child, might be able to do effectively on behalf of all humanity that could not be accomplished by great nations, great religions or private enterprise, no matter how rich or powerfully armed.

I started out fifty-six years ago, at the age of 32, to make that experiment. By good fortune I had acquired a comprehensive experience in commanding and handling ships, first as a sailor in Penobscot Bay, Maine, and later as a regular U.S. naval officer. The navy is inherently concerned with not only all the world's oceans, but also the world's dry land emanating exportable resources and import necessities and the resulting high seas commerce. The navy is concerned with all vital statistics. I saw that there was nothing to stop me from thinking about our total planet Earth and thinking realistically about how to operate it on an enduringly sustainable basis as the magnificent human-passengered spaceship that it is.

Planet Earth is a superbly conceived and realized 6,586,242,500,000,000,000,000-ton (over 6.5 sextillion tons) spaceship, cruise-speeding frictionlessly and soundlessly on an incredibly accurate celestial course. Spaceship Earths spherical passenger deck is largely occupied by a 140-million-square-mile "swimming pool," whose three principal widenings are called oceans.

Upon the surface of the "swimming pool," humanity is playing high-profit gambling games with oil-loaded ships. The largest of all such ships in all history is a quarter-mile-long tanker of 580,000 tons. At top speed it can cross the 3,000-mile-wide Atlantic Ocean in six days. That 3,000-mile, six-day tanker distance is traveled every two and one-half minutes by the eleven-quadrillion-times-heavier Spaceship Earth, which has been moving at this fast rate for at least seven billion years with no signs of slowing or "running out of gas."

As it travels around the Sun at 66,000 m.p.h., it also rotates at an equatorial velocity of 1,000 m.p.h.

The units of time and energy expenditures as "matter" or "work" necessary to structure, equip, and operate all the transcendent-to-human contrivings, biological and chemical organisms and equipment, and their "natural" operational events, including the time-energy units invested in creating and operating volcanoes, earthquakes, seaquakes, and tornadoes, as well as to accomplish this fully equipped and complexedly passengered planet Earth's 66,000 m.p.h. cosmic-highway-traveling speed, stated in the terms of time and energy expended per each ton-mile accomplished at that speed, produces a numerical figure of a staggering magnitude of energy expending.

This staggering energy-expenditure figure for operating planet Earth is in turn utterly belittled when compared to the sum of the same units of time-energy expenditures for structuring, equipping, integrally operating, and moving all of the asteroids, moons, and planets as well as the stars themselves of each of all the known approximately 100 billion other star systems of our Milky Way galaxy, as well as of all the asteroids, moon, and planets, and stars of all the approximately 100 billion star systems of each of all the other two billion galaxies thus far discovered by Earthians to be present and complexedly interacting and co-intershunting with Spaceship Earth in our astro-episode neighborhood of eternally regenerative scenario Universe.

All of these "really real" cosmic energy expenditures may be dramatically compared with, and their significance considered in respect to the fact that, the total of all energy used daily – 95 percent wastefully by all humans for all purposes aboard Spaceship Earth amounts to less than one-millionth of 1 percent of Spaceship Earth's daily income of expendable energy imported from the Universe around and within us.

A vast overabundance of this Earthian cosmic energy income is now technically impoundable and distributable to humanity by presently proven technology. We are not allowed to enjoy this primarily because taxhungry government bureaucracies and moneydrunk big business can't figure a way of putting meters between these cosmic energy sources and the Earthian passengers, so nothing is done about it.

The technical equipment – steel plows, shovels, wheelbarrows, boilers, copper tubing, etc. – essential to individuals' successful harvesting of their own cosmic energy income cannot be economically produced in the backyard kitchen, garage, or studio without the large scale industrial tools' production elsewhere of industrial materials and tools-that-make-tools involving vast initial capital investments. If big business and big government don't want to amass and make available adequate capital for up-to-date technological tooling, people will rarely be able to tap the cosmic energy income, except by berry-, nut-, mushroom-, or applepicking and by fishing.

Volumetrically, S.S. Earth is a 256-billion-cubic-mile spherical vessel of 8,000-miles beam (diameter), having at all times 100 million of its approximately 200 million square miles of spherical surface always exposed to the Sun – with the other hemisphere always in nighttime shadow – bringing about enormous atmospheric, temperature, and pressure differentials and all their resultant high-low weather-produced winds that create all the waves thunderously crashing on all the trillions of miles of our around-the-world shorelines. The atmospheric temperature differentials in turn induce the electromagnetic potential differentials that transform the atmosphere into rain-and lightning-charged clouds from Sun-evaporated waters of the three-fourths-ocean-and-sea-covered Earth.

Gravity's ability to hold together the planet itself, its waters, its biosphere, and other protective mantles, as well as to pull the rain to Earth, thus combines with the photosynthetic capability of the Earth's vast vegetation to harvest solar radiation and store its energies in a manner readily and efficiently convertible into alcohols. The alcohols (four types) constitute the "Grand Central Reservoir" of cosmic-radiation and gravity-generated energy in its most immediately-convertible-into-human-use state – for instance, as high-octane motor fuels, synthetic rubber, and all other products misnamed "petro-chemical products" by their exploiters, whose petroleum is in reality a time-, pressure-, and heat-produced by-product of alcohol.

Radiation is disintegrating because it is held together only at this end of each of its energy-manifesting vectors. Disintegrating, the vectors can be angularly aimed, ergo focused.

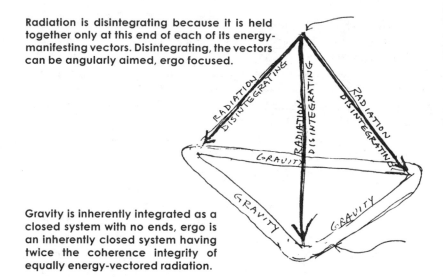

Gravity is inherently integrated as a closed system with no ends, ergo is an inherently closed system having twice the coherence integrity of equally energy-vectored radiation.

Since destruction of humans in Universe would by our working assumption seem to be cosmically undesirable and to be accomplishable only by the anti-intelligent use of the mega-mega-concentrates of energy that humans have learned only recently how to produce and explosively detonate, it is vitally worth our while to stretch our conceptual faculties to understand the physical potentials and possible mystical significance of our most comprehensive inventory of cosmological and cosmoglogical information.

The omni-conserved, nonsimultaneously intertransforming energies of eternally regenerative Universe consist most simply of a plurality of omnimagnitude syntropic convergences here and entropic divergences there. The syntropic convergences integrate as matter. The entropic divergences disintegrate as radiation. The convergently associative function is gravitationally integrative and inherently nondivisible and nondifferentiable until convergently realized as matter.

The radiated disintegration of matter, on the other hand, is inherently differentiable and subdivisible, ergo assignable to a plurality of distinctly separated, vastly remote interminglings with illions of other systems entropically separated-out atomic constituents, thereafter individually to intermingle tentatively and in progressive syntropy as one of myriads of entirely new star systems.

Radiation is inherently focusable and shadowable; gravity is inherently nonfocusable and shadowless. All the stars are atomic-energy-generating "plants." The star Sun is a hydrogen-into-helium intertransformative regenerator of radiation. The sun operates internally at a heat of 26,000,000 degrees Centigrade – a scale on which o degrees represents the freezing point and 100 degrees the boiling point of water.

The cosmic design problem – with the solution of which we are now concerned – was that of employing a safe way of providing the right amount of exclusively star-emanating energy for developing and maintaining the critical-function-in-Universe-serving humans on the only planet having the right environment for both protecting and ecologically supporting those delicately, intricately designed humans, together with their physically and metaphysically critical functionings.

The next star nearest to planet Earth – beyond the Sun – is 300,000 times farther away from the Earth than is the Sun. In solving the "humans on Earth problem, it was therefore necessary to employ the cosmic facilities in such a manner as to transmit the appropriate amount of the specific radiation constituents in nonlethal concentration from the Sun, the star nearest to the human-incubating planet Earth – the planet having not only the most propitious environmental condition for humanity incubating, but also maintaining the exact vast complex of close-tolerance-of-physical-error limits within which humans could survive.

Humans cannot impound enough energy by sunbathing to keep them alive and operative. Planet Earth's safe importing of Sun radiation must first be impoundingly accomplished by vegetation in energy quantities adequate to supporting not only the vegetation and the humans but all the other myriads of species of life altogether constituting the regenerative ecologic system. To do this, the angular fan-out concentration of energy intensity must be accomplished by attaining adequate distance from the Sun, and thereby to arrive at protoplasmically tolerable increments of energy exactly sustained for conversion by botanical photosynthesis into hydrocarbon molecules, which thereafter can be assimilated metabolically by all other living biological organisms. This means that the Sun's surface energy radiation must be transformingly programmed to angularly deconcentrate during its eight-minute, 92-million-mile passage from Sun to Earth to arrive in nonlethal increments and at nonlethal temperatures.

The farther away a cosmic radiation source is, the less concentrated the radiation. Only about one-billionth of the radiation given off omnidirectionally by the Sun is so aimed as to impinge directly upon the surface of planet Earth.

With all the space of Universe to work with, the great designing wisdom of Universe seems to have found it to be essential that the energy organized as the predominantly water-structured substance that is all biological life be maintained at a distance apparently never greater than 95 million miles and never less than 91 million miles away from the atomic-energy-generating plant of the Sun's initial magnitude of radiation concentration.

Sad to say, those of the present Earthian power-structure's scientists who assert that they can safely bury atomic radiation wastes within the ever-transforming structure of planet Earth are rationalizing information critical to human continuance aboard planet Earth. They and their only-selfishly-motivated masters are gambling the future of all humanity to win only the continuing increase of their personal economic power control for the few remaining years of only their own lives.

While the totality of atomic wastes now Earth-buried or ocean-sunk is as yet of a feasibly rocketable total bulk and weight for a plurality of blastings-off, we may still send such atomic wastes back into the Sun where they can once more become safely exportable.

Humans who think they are better designers than God are the most to be pitied of liars-the liars who are believingly convinced by their own only-self-conveniencing fabrications.

On rereading what I have just said about humans falsifying critical information, I am retrospectively shocked at my making those two negative citations.

Firstly, my positive information, which if comprehended can help toward realization of physical success for humanity, when followed by my negativism, reduces the credibility of my wisdom and thereby reduces the value of my positive information.

Secondly, we observe from experience that nature has its own checks and balances, accelerators and brakes, temporary side-tracking, overload circuit breakers, self-starters, transformers, birth and death rates, and complex overall evolutionary gestation rates.

Natures biggest, most important problems take the longest to solve satisfactorily because they can be solved only by lessons humanly learned through trial-and-error mistake-making; and, most important, by those who make the mistakes and their self-recognition and public acknowledgment of their errors and their only-thereby-learned-from positive clues to effective solutions of evolutionary problems in the present instance, the problem of how best to abruptly terminate further atomic energy development for human use as fissionally or fusionally generated aboard planet Earth. The problem is one of immediate and direct concern to each individual of our four billion humans, as well as to all the potential many yet to be born and to God. Its satisfactory solution can be arrived at only through major design-science initiative-takings that produce far superior technologies to render spontaneously obsolete the previous undesirable technology.

Vividly, I recall an occasion when I was about ten and my father heard me call my own brother a fool. My father said, "Bucky, I do not take everything I read as being reliable, not even when I read it in the Bible. But I find by experience that statements in the Bible are far more often reliable than are declarations printed elsewhere. There is a statement in the Bible that you should remember: he who calls his brother a fool shall be in danger of hell's fire.

In these critical times let us no longer make the mistake of identifying as fools those with whom we disagree.

The late twentieth century's confused, fearful human chitchat about an Earthian energy crisis discloses the abysmal state of ignorance within which we Earthians now struggle. All this results in realization of the almost absolute futility of the disintegrated ways in which humanity's present leaders cope with this one-and-only-available Spaceship Earth and its one-and-only-available Universe and with the problems of human survival, let alone attainment of physical success for all humanity within the critical time limit.

For all those who wished to observe them – I being one such person – all the foregoing concepts were already apparent in 1927, though in far less obvious degree. The sum of all these facts made it clear to me in 1927 that no matter how much I could, did, or might as yet accomplish, as a human problem-solver employing only an artifact-designed industrial-production revolution on Spaceship Earth – seeking by techno-economic obsolescence, rather than by political reform, to make physically obsolete all ignorantly incapacitating reflexing of humanity – I could not possibly make more of a mess-of-it-all than that being made by the behind-the-scenes absolutely selfish world power-structures' puppeting of the 150 "sovereign" prime ministers, their national legislatures, and their in-turn-puppeted generals and admirals, and the latter's omni-intercompetitive commanding of our one-and-only spaceship, with each five-star "admiral general" looking out only for his own sovereignly-escutcheoned stateroom and all the starboard-side admirals trying to find a way of sinking all the port-side admirals without the winning admirals getting their own feet wet, let alone being drowned.

I saw that there was nothing to stop me from studying – hopefully to discover, comprehend, and eventually employ design-wise – the integrated total family of generalized principles by which nature operates this magnificent, human-passengered, spherical spaceship as entirely enclosed within an external set of physically unique, spherically concentric environmental zones altogether producing the critically complex balance of intertransformative energy conditions essential to maintaining an omniregenerative planetary ecology – all accomplished in local Universe support of eternally omni-interregenerative Universe itself by means of planet Earths syntropic, biochemical capability to photosynthetically convert stellar radiation (primarily that of the Sun) into hydrocarbon-structured vegetation that in turn is converted as "food" into all manner of biological proliferatings, ultimately after aeons of enormous heat and pressure treatment produced by deep-Earth burial – to be converted into fossil fuels.

This Earthian energy impounding and conserving altogether constitutes a cosmic accumulation of energy ultimately adequate – billions of years hence – to produce "critical mass" for self-starting its own "all-out" atomic energy generators and thus itself becoming a radiation-exporting star.

I saw that this planet Earth's organic-biochemical interstructuring is (1) tensionally produced only by triple-bonded, no-degrees-of-freedom, crystalline interarrayings of atomic events, (2) compressionally structured only by double-bonded, flexibly jointed, pressure-distributing and omni-stress-equalizing, hydraulic interarrangements of atomic events, and (3) shock-absorbingly structured, singlebondedly and pneumatically, by gaseous interarrangement of atomic events.

I saw that approximately one-half of all the mobile biological structuring consists of water, which freezes and boils within very close thermal-environment limits, the physical accommodation of which limiting requirements is uniquely maintained in Universe only within the biosphere of Spaceship Earth that is, so far as human information goes.

And I repeat for emphasis that I saw in 1927 that there was nothing to stop me from trying to think about how and why humans are here as passengers aboard this spherical spaceship we call Earth. Return to this initial question has always produced for me the most relevant and incisive of insights. Therefore I hope all humanity will begin to ask itself this question in increasingly attentive earnestness. I also saw that there was nothing to stop me from thinking about the total physical resources we have now discovered aboard our ship and about how to use the total cumulative know-how to make this ship work for everybody paying absolutely no attention to the survival problems of any separate nations or any other individual groupings of humans, and assuming only one goal: the omni-physically successful, spontaneous self-integration of all humanity into what I called in 1927 "a one-town world."

I knew at the 1927 outset that this was to be a very long-distance kind of search, research, and development experiment, probably to take at least one-half a century to bring to fruition, with no capital backing. At any rate, I want you to understand now why I had no competition undertaking to solve all human physio-economic problems only by an environment-improving, artifact inventing-and-developing revolution, which inadvertently produced its recognition by the media, which incidental news publishing is the only reason you know about me – especially since I have been only inadvertently producing news-provoking artifacts for fifty-six years. All that news has failed to induce any sincerely sustained realistic competition with my efforts and on my economic premise of non-money-making but hopefully sense-making – and only-by-faith-in-God-sustained objectives.

Because it was a very large undertaking, I didn't know that I would be here to see it through for all those 56 years. I was born in 1895. The life insurance companies' actuarial life-expectancy for me was 42 years. I was already 32 when I started the project. I have been amazed that things have worked out to the extent that they have, that I am as yet vigorously active, and that I have been able to find so many relevant things that a little individual can do that a great nation and capital enterprise can't do.

Yet I am quite confident there is nothing that I have undertaken to do that others couldn't do equally well or better under the same economic circumstances. I was supported only by my faith in God and my vigorously pursued working assumption that it is God's intent to make humans an economic success so that they can and may in due course fulfill an essential – and only mind-renderable – functioning in Universe.

Assuming this to be God's intent, I saw that if I committed myself only to initiating, inventing, and full-scale prototyping of life-protecting and -supporting artifacts that afforded ever more inclusive, efficient, and in every way more humanly pleasing performances while employing ever less pounds of materials, ergs of energy, and seconds of time per each accomplished function, a young public's enthusiasm for acquisition of those artifacts and youth's increasing satisfaction with the services thereby produced might induce their further development and multiplication by other significance-comprehending and initiative-taking young humans.

I saw that this ever-multiplying activity could lead ultimately to full-scale, world-around, only-for-industrial-mass-production-prototyped artifacts. I saw that this mass-production-and-distribution of livingry service could provide an adequate inventory of public-attention-winning-and-supporting artifacts, efficient and comprehensive enough to swiftly provide the physical success for all humanity. This would terminate humanity's need to "earn a living," i.e., doing what others wanted done only for others' ultimately selfish reasons. This attending only to what needs to be done for all humanity in turn would allow humanity the time to effectively attend to the Universe-functioning task for the spontaneous performance of which God – the eternal, comprehensive, intellectual integrity usually referred to as "nature" or as "evolution" – had included humans in the grand design of eternally regenerative Universe.

It was clear to me that if my scientifically reasoned working assumptions were correct and if I did my part in successfully initiating, and following-through on realizing, the previously recited potential chain-reactive events, I would be supported by God in realistic, natural, but almost always utterly surprising-to-me ways. I therefore committed myself to such initiations, realizations, and followings-through.

Because I knew at the 1927 outset of the commitment that no one else thought my commitment to be practical or profitable, I also knew that no one would keep any record of its evolvement should it be so fortunate as to evolve. Since I intended to do everything in a comprehensively scientific manner in committing myself to this very large-scale experiment (which, as already stated, sought to discover what a little, unknown, moneyless, creditless individual with dependents could do effectively on behalf of all humanity that – inherently could never be done by any nations or capital enterprise), I saw clearly that I must keep my own comprehensive records – records being a prime requisite of scientific exploration. This I have done. It has been expensive and difficult both to accomplish and to maintain. It is comprehensive and detailed. I speak of the record as the "archives." They consist of:

A. The "Chronofile," which in 1981 consisted of 750 12" x 10" x 5" volumes. These volumes contain all my correspondence, as well as sketches and doodles made during meetings with others, and also back-of-envelope and newspaper-edged notes, all maintained chronologically – in exact order of inbound and outbound happenings – all the way from my earliest childhood to the present keeping of such records as induce discovery of what to avoid in future initiatives

B. All the drawings and blueprints I have been able to save of all the design and full-scale artifact-inventing, -developing and -testing realizations

C. All the economically retainable models

D. All the moving picture and television footage covering my work

E. All the wire and tape recorded records of my public addresses

F. All the affordable news-bureau and clipping-service records of articles or books written by others about me or my work

G. All the posters announcing my lecturing appearances as designed and produced by others

H. A large conglomeration of items (for instance, over 100 T-shirts with pictures of my work or quotations of my public utterances) produced and distributed by students at many of the 550 universities and colleges that have invited me to speak; collection of awards, mementos, etc.

I. All the multi-stage copies of the manuscript and typescript versions of my twenty-three formally published books and many published magazine articles

J. Over 10,000 4" x 5" photo negatives and over 30,000 photographs, all code-listed, covering my life and work; also 20,000 35-mm projection slides

K. My own extensive library of relevant books and published articles

L. All my financial records, including annual income tax returns

M. All the indexes to the archival material

N. All the drafting tools, typewriters, computers, furniture, and file cabinets for an office staff of seven

O. A large collection of framed photos, paintings, diplomas, cartoons, etc.

P. Biographical data, published periodically (approximately every three years), summarizing all developments of my original commitments

Q. The "Inventory of World Resources, Human Trends and Needs"

R. The World Game records

The archives' collected public record now consists of over 100,000 newspaper and magazine articles, books, and radio and television broadcasts about me or my work, unsolicitedly conceived and produced by other human beings all around the world since 1917.

The prime public record of my more-than-half-century's fulfillment of my commitment has been realized in the working artifacts themselves – the 300,000 world-around geodesic domes, the five million Dymaxion World Maps, the many thousands of copies of each of my twenty-three published books – and, most important of all, within the minds and memories of the 30,000 students I have taught how to think about how to design socially needed, more efficiently produced artifacts.

I do not now employ, and never have employed, any professional public relations agents or agencies, lecture or publishing bureaus, salespeople, sales agencies, or promotional workers. As indicated earlier, I am convinced that nature has her own conceptioning, gestation, birth, development, maturization, and death rates, the magnitudes of which vary greatly in respect to the biochemistry and technological arts involved. The most important evolutionary events take the longest.

Since maintenance of the updating and safety of the archives is as yet my responsibility, they are not open to the public, though scholars from time to time are allowed to view them and be shown items of special interest to them. Because I avoid employing any professional agencies, the magnitude of my development is not kept track of and publicly reported by any of the professional agency associations. For instance, I am not included in the annual statements appearing in the news regarding the public speakers most in demand. Therefore every three years or so my office updates my "basic biography," as it is called, to be distributed to those who ask for information.

Because we are now entering upon the 1927-initiated half-century period of realization, it is now appropriate to make public exposure of the record in order to encourage youth to undertake its own mind-evolved initiatives.

I am therefore publishing herewith:

1. A compilation of my U.S. patents, with photographs of each of the realized artifacts covered by each patent.

2. The compendium of honorary doctorate citations. Since I did not graduate from any college or university and since I have not amassed riches and made generous financial gifts to the schools, I am confident that none of the doctorates were conferred upon me as a financial benefactor but only in recognition of my on-campus academic activities, as a visiting lecturer, a research project initiator and director, or as an appointed professor. Here my work could be intimately judged for its educational value, wherefore the awarding of honorary doctorate degrees to me constitutes an objective assessment of the magnitude and validity of my working knowledge and of its usefulness to the educational system and society. Like the public record established by my patents, these doctorates can serve as critical appraisal of the historical relevance, practicality, and relative effectiveness of my half-century's experimental commitment to discover what, if anything, an individual human eschewing politics and money-making can do effectively on behalf of all humanity.

I hope that the record so documented (and your hoped-for-by-me close examination of it) will serve as an encouragement to you as individuals to undertake tasks that you can see need to be attended to, which are not to the best of your knowledge being attended to by others, and for which there are no capital backers. You are going to have to test a cosmic intellectual integrity as being inherently manifest in the eternally generalized scientific and only mathematically expressible laws governing the complex design of Universe and of all the myriads of objective special-case realizations.

I am presenting all these thoughts and records because I think we are coming to a very extraordinary moment in the history of humanity, when only such a spontaneous, competent, and ultimately cooperative design-science initiative-taking, on the part of a large majority of human individuals, can ensure humanity's safe crossing of the cosmically critical threshold into its prime and possibly eternal functioning in the macro-micro cosmic scheme.

All humans have always been born naked, completely helpless for months, beautifully equipped but with no experience, therefore absolutely ignorant. This is a very important design fact. I do not look at such a human start as constituting a careless or chance oversight in the cosmic conceptioning of the intellectual integrity governing the Universe. The initial ignorance of humans was by deliberate cosmic (divine) design.

We know that before humans are born forth, naked from their mothers' wombs, their protoplasmic cells are chromosomally (DNA-RNA) programmed to produce each human in incredibly successful regenerative detail.

If we study both the overall integrated system and the detail-design features of our own physical organism – for instance, our optical system and its intimacy with our brain's nervous system – we realize what miraculously complex yet eminently successful anticipatory-design-science phenomena are the humans and the cosmic totality of our complex supportive environment.

If I accidentally scratch-cut myself when I am 3, nature goes instantly to work and repairs the cut. I don't know, even now at 88, how to repair my own cell-structured tissue, and I certainly didn't know how at 3 years of age. We understand very little. Obviously, however, we are magnificently successful products of design in a Universe the complexity and intricacy of whose design integrity utterly transcends human comprehension, let alone popularly acceptable descriptions of "divine design."

Photo by Wernber Krutein/Photovault.com

Photo by Wernber Krutein/Photovault.com

Photo by Wernber Krutein/Photovault.com

Therefore the fact that we are designed to be born naked, helpless, and ignorant is, I feel, a very important matter. We must pay attention to that. We are also designed to be very hungry and to be continually rehungered and rethirsted and multiplyingly curious. Therefore we are quite clearly designed to be inexorably driven to learn only by trial and error how to get on in life. As a consequence of the design, we have had to make an incredible number of mistakes, that being the only way we can find out "what's what" and a little bit about "why," and an even more meager bit regarding "how" we can take advantage of what we have learned from our mistakes.

Suppose a hypothetical 3-billion-B.C. "you," being enormously hungry, ate some invitingly succulent red berries and was poisoned. The tribe concluded, "Berries are poisonous. People can't eat berries." And for the next thousand years, that tribe did not do so. Then along came somebody who showed them they could safely eat blueberries.

At any rate it took a long, long time for humanity to get to the point where it was inventing words with which to integrate and thereby share the lessons individually learned from error-inducing experiences. Humans could help one another only by confessing what each had found out only by trial and error. Most often "know-it-all" ego blocked the process.

After inventing spoken words, humanity took a long time more to invent writing, with which both the remote-from-local-community and the dead gave the remote-from-one-another beings information about their remote-in-time-and-space error-discovering and truth-uncovering experience. Thus does evolution continually compound the wisdom accruing to error-making and - discovering experiences, the self-admission of which alone can uncover that which is true.

Informed by the senses, the brains of all creatures unthinkingly reflex in pursuing only the sensorially obvious and attractive wilderness trails, waterways, and mountain passes along which may exist fallen-leaves-hidden pit-falls.

This fact made possible the effectiveness of the pitfall trap – falling into the pit at 90 degrees to the 180 degrees line of sight spontaneously followed in pursuit of the obvious. This straightaway reflexing is frequently employed by nature to give humans an opportunity to learn that which humanity needs to learn if humanity is ever to attain the capability to perform its cosmically assigned, spontaneous, intellectually responsible functioning. If ego is surmounted, mind may discover and comprehend the significance of the negative event and may thereby discover the principles leading not only to escape from the entrapment but discovery of what is truly worthwhile pursuing, but only as a consequence of the mind's exclusive capability to discover and employ not just one principle but the synergetically interoperative significance of all the human mind's thus-far-discovered principles.

Up to a very short time ago – that is to say, up to the twentieth century – humans were only innately wise but comprehensively information-ignorant. We have had to discover many errors to become reasonably intelligent.

For instance, when I was young those humans who were most remote from others had to travel a minimum of six months to reach one another; approximately none of them ever did so. That is why Kipling's "East is East, and West is West, and never the twain shall meet" seemed so obviously true to the vast millions who read or heard his words. That has all changed. Today, any one of us having enough credit to acquire a jet air-transport ticket can – using only scheduled flights – physically reach anybody else around the world within twenty-four hours, or can reach each other by telephone within minutes.

The furthestmost point away from any place on our approximately 25-thousand-mile-circumferenced Earth sphere is always halfway around the world, which is 12,500 great-circle miles away in any direction from the point at which we start. Flying the shortest distance from the exact North Pole to the South Pole, any direction you first head in will be "due south." If you keep on heading exactly south you will find yourself following a one-great-circle meridian of longitude until you get to the South Pole. Furthermore, to reach your halfway-around-the-Earth, furthest-away-from-you point which is always 12,500 miles away – flying in a Concorde supersonic transport, cruising efficiently at Mach 2 (approximately 1,400 m.p.h.), and including stopover refueling times, you will reach that furthestmost halfway-around-the-world-from-where-you-started point in half a day.

Humanity, which yesterday was remotely deployed by evolution, is now being deliberately integrated to make us all very intimate with one another and probably ultimately to crossbreed us back into one physically similar human family.

When I was young we were extremely ignorant about other people. I was told that people even in the next town were very dangerous: they "drink whiskey and have knives…, you had better not go over there." I was 7 years old when the first automobile came into Boston. When the owner of one of those excitingly new 1902 automobiles drove me over into one of those "dangerous" next towns, I could see no one who appeared to be more "dangerously threatening" than any of my very nonthreatening hometown neighbors.

I was 8 when the Wright brothers first flew. I was 12 when we had the first public wireless telegraphy. I was 19 when we had our first "world" war.

I was born in an almost exclusively walking-from-here-to-there world, a Victorian world in which we knew nothing about strangers. The assumption was that all strangers were inherently unreliable people. When I was young, 95 percent of all humans were illiterate. Today over 60 percent of the times as many humans present on Earth are literate. All this has happened unpredictedly in only one lifetime. The majority of older humans of today are as yet apprehensive of strangers and pretend nonrecognition while the majority of those 30 years and younger tend to welcome strangers, often with open arms.

Something very big has been going on in my particular generation's lifetime where all the fundamental conditions of humanity are changing at an ever-accelerating acceleration rate.

When I was young, not only were 95 percent of human beings illiterate but their speech patterns were also atrociously difficult to understand. I had two jobs before World War I. The men I worked with were very skilled but their awkwardly articulated, ill-furnished vocabularies were limited to about 100 words 50 percent of them blasphemous or obscene. Primarily they let you know how they felt about matters by the way in which they spit – delightedly, amusedly, approvingly, or disgustedly. They were wonderfully lovable and brave human beings but that swearing and spitting was the most articulate and effective expressive language they had. Their pronunciations varied not only from town to town and from one part of a town to another but also from house to house and from individual to individual.

Something extraordinary has happened. Only within our last-of-the-twentieth-century time, approximately everybody has acquired a beautiful vocabulary. This did not come from the schooling system but from the radio and TV, where the people who secured the performing jobs did so by virtue of their common pronunciation, the clarity of their speech, and the magnitude of their vocabularies. They no longer spoke with the myriad of esoteric pronunciations of yesterday. People were introduced to a single kind of language. This brought about primary common-speech patterns. The necessity for pilots of airplanes operating daily around the world from countries all around the world to have a common language has swiftly evolved into a common language. Olympic Games, athletics in general, and frequently televised world affairs have all been accelerating the coming of a to-be evolved world language. That the language most commonly used in 1983 is English is unfortunate and untrue. What we call English was not the language of long-ago-vanished Angles and Jutes. It is the most crossbred of all the world-around languages of all the world-around people who on their ever westwardly and mildly northwestwardly colonizing way have historically invaded or populated England. "English" now includes words from all the world's languages and represents an agglomeration of the most frequently used and most easily pronounceable words.

Since throughout at least three million years people did not understand languages well, they were relatively ignorant. Their group survival required leaders. Thus through the comprehensively illiterate ages we came historically to require powerful leaders – sometimes as physical warriors, sometimes as spiritual warriors, sometimes as unique individual personalities. Statesmen steered great religious organizations or great government organizations that led the affairs of illiterate, uninformed humanity.

We have come now to a completely new moment in the history of humans at which approximately everybody is "in" on both speech and information.

Humanity has been coming out of a group-womb of permitted ignorance made possible only by the existence of an enormous cushion of natural physical resources with which to learn only by trial and error, thus to become somewhat educated about how and why humans happen to be here on this planet. Despite a doubling of world population during my lifetime, humanity has at the same time gone from 95 percent illiterate to 60 percent literate.

Until I was 28 we Earthians knew only about our own Milky Way galaxy. In 1923 Hubble discovered another galaxy. Since that time we have discovered two billion more of them. That explosively accelerated rate of expansion of our astronomical-information-acquisitioning typifies the rate of popular increase of both scientifically general and technically special information during my lifetime.

We are living in a new evolutionary moment in which the human is being individually educated to do the free-standing human's own thinking, and each is thereby separately becoming extraordinarily well informed. We have reached a threshold moment where the individual human beings are in what I consider to be a "final examination" as to whether they, individually, as a cosmic invention, are to graduate successfully into their mature cosmic functioning or, failing, are to be classified as "imperfects" and "discontinued items" on this planet and anywhere else in Universe.

We are at a human examination point at which it is critically necessary for each of us individually to have some self-discovered, logically reasonable, experience-engendered idea of how and why we are here on this little planet in this star system and galaxy, amongst the billions of approximately equally star-populated galaxies of Universe. I assume it is because human minds were designed with the capability to discover from time to time the only-mathematically-stateable principles governing the eternal interrelationships existing between various extraordinary phenomena – a capability possessed by no known phenomenon other than humans.

How and why were we given our beautiful minds with their exclusive access to the scientific principles governing the operational design of eternally regenerative Universe?

As an instance of the human mind's capability, we have the integration of the unplanned, only evolutionarily combined works of Copernicus, Kepler, and Galileo informedly inspiring Isaac Newton into assuming hypothetically that the interattractiveness of any two celestial bodies varies inversely as of the second power of the arithmetical distances intervening if you double the arithmetical distance intervening, you will reduce the interattractiveness to one-fourth what it had been. Astronomers applied his hypothesis to their celestial observations and discovered that this mathematical formulation explained the ever-mobile interpositioning behaviors of all known and measuringly-observed celestial bodies. Thus, Newton's hypothesis became adopted as a "scientifically generalized law."

In dramatic contradistinction to the brain's functioning within only directly nerve-sensing limits, the human mind has the capability, once in a great while, to discover invisible, soundless, unsmellable, untasteable, untouchable interrelationships eternally existing between separate, special-case cosmic entities, which eternal interrelationships are not manifest by any of the interested entities when considered only separately and which interrelationships can be expressed only mathematically and constitute eternal cosmic laws – such as Newton's discovery that the interattractiveness existing invisibly between any two celestial bodies always varies inversely as the second power of the arithmetically expressed distances intervenes those bodies. Such Universal laws can be expressed only mathematically. Mathematics, we note, is purely intellectual. Altogether these laws manifest the eternal intellectual integrity of Universe that I speak of as "God."

Human intellect (mind) has gradually discovered a number of these extraordinary, generalized, non-sensorially-apprehensible eternal principles. We human beings have been given access to at least some of the design laws of the Universe.

We don't know of any other phenomenon that has such a faculty and such an access permit, wherefore we may assume that we humans must be cosmically present for some very, very important reason.

As far as I know, we humans haven't thought or talked very much about how and why we are here as either a desirable or a necessary function of Universe. We have talked a great deal about the great mystery of being here. But the majority of our public talking centers on the egotistical assumption that human politics and the wealthy are running the Universe, that the macrocosmic spectaculars are an accessory amusement of our all-important selfish preoccupations, and that Universe's microcosmic invisibles are exclusively for corporate stockholders' money-making exploitation – though always individually discovered or invented but only industrially developed, funded exclusively by the research departments of great corporations as initially funded by humanity's taxes-paid military defense expenditures after production rights are transferred to prime corporations.

We humans are overwhelmed because we are so tiny and the Earth is so big and the celestial systems so vast. It is very hard for us to think effectively and realistically about what we feel about the significance of all we have learned about Universe.

At any rate, we are now at a point where we have to begin to think realistically about how and why we are here with this extraordinary capability of the mind. Our remaining here on Earth isn't a matter of the cosmic validity of any Earthian economic systems, political systems, religious systems, or other mystical-organization systems. Our "final examination" is entirely a matter of each of all the individual human beings, all of whom have been given this extraordinary, truly divine capability of the mind, individually qualifying in their own right to continue in Universe as an extraordinary thinking faculty. If all of humanity as a cosmic invention is to successfully pass this final examination, it would seem to be logically probable that a large majority of all Earthian individuals make and do the passing for themselves and for the remaining numbers.

Are we individually going to be able to break out from our institutionally misconditioned reflexing? Are we going to be able to question intelligently all the things that we have been taught only to believe and not to expose to the experiential-evidence tests? Are we going to really dare to make our own behavioral strategy decisions as informed only by our own separate experimentally or experientially derived evidence? The integrity of individually thinking human beings – as mind vs. brain-reflexing automatons is being tested.

My own working assumption of why we are here is that we are here as local-Universe information-gatherers and that we are given access to the divine design principles so that we can therefrom objectively invent instruments and tools – e.g., the microscope and the telescope – with which to extend all sensorial inquiring regarding the rest of the to-the-naked-eye-invisible, micro-macro Universe, because human beings, tiny though we are, are here for all the local-

Universe information-harvesting and cosmic-principle-discovering, objective tool-inventing, and local-environment-controlling as local Universe problem-solvers in support of the integrity of eternally regenerative Universe.

To fulfill our ultimate cosmic functioning we needed the telescope and microscope, having only within the present century discovered that almost all the Universe is invisible. I was two years old when the electron was discovered. That began a new era. When I entered Harvard my physics text had a yellow-paper appendix that had just been glued into the back of the white-leaved physics book. The added section was called "Electricity." The vast ranges of the invisible reality of Universe constituted a very new world – for humanity, a very different kind of world.

When I was born, "reality" was everything you could see, smell, touch, and hear. That's all there was to it. But suddenly we extended our everyday doings and thinkings, not linearly but omnidirectionally into the vast outward, macro-ranges and inwardly penetrating to discover the infra-micro-tune-in-able ranges of the invisible within-ness world.

We began to discover all kinds of new chemical, biological, and electromagnetic behaviors of the invisible realm so that today 99.999 percent of the search and research for everything that is going to affect all our lives tomorrow is being conducted in the realm of reality nondirectly contactable by the human senses. It takes a really educated human to be able to cope with the vast and exquisite ranges of reality.

So here we are – as human beings – majorly educated and individually endowed with developable capabilities of getting on successfully within the invisible ultra-macro and infra-micro world.

Here we have found that each chemical element has its own electromagnetic spectrum wavelengths and frequencies that are absolutely unique to that particular element-isotope. These wavelengths and frequencies are nondirectly tune-in-able by the human senses but are all spectroscopically differentiable and photographically convertible into human readability.

Repeating to emphasize its significance, we note that exploring with the spectroscope, photo-telescope, and radio telescope, humans only recently have traveled informationally to discover about two billion galaxies with an average of 100 billion stars each, all existing within astronomy's present 11.5 billion-light-years' radial reach in all directions of the vastness around us.

Taking all the light from all those galaxies we have been able to discover spectroscopically – and have inventoried here on board planet Earth – the relative interabundance of each of the unique categories of all the chemical elements present within that 11.5 billion-light-years realm around us. That little Earthian humans can accomplish that scale of scientific inventorying makes it possible to realize what the human mind can really do. One can begin to comprehend what God is planning to do with the humans' cosmic functioning.

In our immediate need to discover more about ourselves we also note that what is common to all human beings in all history is their ceaseless confrontation by problems, problems, problems. We humans are manifestly here for problem-solving and, if we are any good at problem-solving, we don't come to utopia, we come to more difficult problems to solve: That apparently is what we're here for, so I therefore conclude that we humans are here for local information-gathering and local problem-solving with our minds having access to the design principles of the Universe and – I repeat – thereby finally discover that we are most probably here for local information-gathering and local-Universe problem-solving in support of the integrity of eternally regenerative Universe.

If our very logically and experientially supported working assumption is right, that is a very extraordinarily important kind of function for which we humans were designed ultimately to fulfill. It is clearly within the premises of the divine.

We note also that when nature has a very important function to perform, such as regenerating Earthian birds to play their part in the overall ecological regenerating, nature doesn't put all her birds' eggs in one basket. Instead she provides myriads of fail-safe alternate means of satisfying each function.

Nature must have illions of alternate solutions in this cosmic locality to serve effectively the local information-gathering and local problem-solving in local support of the integrity of an eternally regenerative Universe – should we humans fail to graduate from our potential lessons-learning games of ever more exquisite micro-invisible discrimination and ever greater political, economic, educational, and religious mistake-making.

When in 1927 I started the experiment to discover what a little individual might be able to do effectively on behalf of all humanity, I said to myself. "You are going to have to do all your own thinking." I had been brought up in an era in which all the older people said to all the young people. "Never mind what you think. Listen to what we are trying to teach you to think!" However, as experience multiplied, I learned time and again that the way things often turned out evidenced that the way I had been thinking was often a more accurate, informative, and significant way of comprehending the significance of events than was the academic and conventional way I was being taught, so I said, "If I am going to discard all my taught-to-believe reflexings, I must do all my own thinking. I must go entirely on my own direct experiential evidence."

I said, "It has been an impressive part of my experience that most human beings have a powerful feeling that there is some greater and more exaltedly benign authority operating in the Universe than that of human beings – a phenomenon they call 'God.' There are many ways of thinking about 'God' and I saw that most children are brought up to 'believe' this and that concerning the subject. By the word believe I mean 'accepting explanations of physical and metaphysical phenomena without any supportive physical evidence, i.e., without reference to any inadvertently experienced information-harvesting or deliberate-experimental-evidence expansion of our knowledge.'"

I then said to myself, "If you are going to give up all the beliefs and are going to have to go only on your own experiential evidence, you are going to have to ask yourself if you have any experience that would cause you to have to say to yourself there is quite clearly a greater intellect operating in the Universe than that of human beings.

Luckily I had had a good scientific training, and the discovery of those great, eternal, scientific principles that could only be expressed mathematically – mathematics is purely intellectual made me conclude that I was overwhelmed with the manifests of a greater intellect operating in Universe than that of humans, which acknowledgment became greatly fortified by the following experiential observations.

Scientific perusal of the personal diaries, notes, and letters written by three of history's most significant scientific discoverers – just before, at the time of, and immediately after the moment of their great discoveries – finds that the written records of all of them, unaware of the others' experiences, make it eminently clear that two successive intuitions always played the principal role in their successful accomplishing of their discoveries: the first intuition telling them that a "fish was nibbling at their baited hook" and the second intuition telling them how to "jerk" their fishing line to "hook" and successfully "land" that fish.

The records of these same three scientists also make clear that to start with there must be human curiosity-arousal followed by an intuition-excitation of the human that causes the individual to say, "There is something very significant going on here regarding which I have yet no specific clues, let alone comprehension, because special-case evidences of generalized principles are always myriadiy and only complexedly manifest in nature." To qualify as a scientifically generalized principle the scientifically observed and measured special-case behavioral manifests of the generalized interrelationship principles must always be experimentally redemonstrable under a given set of explicitly and implicitly controlled conditions.

Scientifically generalized principles must be repeatedly demonstrable as being both exceptionless and only elegantly expressible as simple, three-term mathematical equations, such as $E = mc^2$.

Constantly intercovarying, ever experimentally redemonstrable interrelations, which have no exceptions, are inherently "eternal."

As a consequence of the foregoing, I then said, "Brain is always and only coordinating the information reported to us by our senses regarding both the macro outside world around us and the micro world within us, and recording, recalling, and only reflexively behaving in response to previous similar experiencing if any or if none' to newly imagined safe-way logic. No one has ever seen or in any way directly sensed anything outside the brain. The brain is our smell-, touch-, sound-, and image-ination tele-set whose reliability of objective image formulation has been for all childhood so faithful that we humans soon become convinced that we are sensing directly outside ourselves, whereas the fact is that no one has ever seen or heard or felt or smelt outside themselves. All sensing occurs inside the brain's 'television control zone.' The brain always and only deals with temporal, special-case, human-senses-reported experiences. Mind is always concerned only with multi-reconsidering a host of special-case experiences that have intuitively tantalizing implications of ultimately manifesting the operative presence of an as-yet-to-be-discovered eternal principle governing an invisible, unsmellable, soundless, untouchable eternal interrelationship and that complete interrelationships' possibly to be discovered, constantly covarying interrelationships' rate of change. Such principles, whether discovered or not, are intuitively held to always both embrace and permeate all special-case experiences."

I then said to myself, "I am scientifically convinced that the thus-far-discovered and proven inventory of unfailingly redemonstrable generalized principles are a convincing manifest of an eternal intellect governing the myriad of nonsimultaneously and only overlappingly occurring episodes of finite but non-unitarily conceptual, multi-where and multi-when eternally regenerative scenario Universe.

"In so governing the great Universe's integrity, cosmic intellect always and only designs with the generalized principles that are inherently eternal.

"That all the eternal principles always and only appear to be comprehensively and concurrently operative may prove to be an eternal interrelationship condition, which latter hypothesis is fortified by the fact that none of the eternal principles has ever been found to contradict another. All of the eternal principles appear to be both constantly interaccommodative-intersupportive and multiplyingly interaugmentative.

"When you and I speak of design, we spontaneously think of it as an intellectual conceptualizing event in which intellect first sorts out a plurality of elements and then interarranges them in a preferred way.

Ergo, the "eternal intellect" – the eternal intellectual integrity – apparently governs the integrity of the great design of the Universe and all of its special-case, temporal realizations of the complex interemployments of all the eternal principles."

So I said, "I am overwhelmed by the evidence of an eternally existent and operative, omnicompetent, greater intellect than that of human beings."

Consequently, I also said in 1927, "Here I am launching a half-century-magnitude program with nobody telling me to do so, or suggesting how to do it." I had absolutely no money and my darling wife (who has now been married to me for 66 years) was willing to go along with my thinking and commitments. I said to myself, "If I, in confining my activity to inventing, proving and improving, and physically producing artifacts suggested to me by physical challenges of the a priori environment, which inventions alter the environment consistently with evolution's trending, whereby I am doing that which is compatible with what universal evolution seems intent upon doing – which is to say, if I am doing what God wants done, i.e., employing my mind to help other humans' minds to render all humanity a physically self-regenerative and comprehensively intellectual integrity success so that humans can effectively give their priority of attention to the ongoing local Universe information-gathering and local problem-solving, primarily with design-science artifact solutions which will altogether result in comprehensive environmental transformation leading to conditions so favorable to humans' physical wellbeing and metaphysical equanimity as to permit humans to become permanently engaged with only the by-mind-conceived challenges of local Universe – then I do not have to worry about not being commissioned to do so by any Earthians and I don't have to worry how we are going to acquire the money, tools, and services necessary to produce the successively evoluting special-case physical artifacts that will most effectively increase humanity's technological functioning advantage to an omnisuccess-producing degree."

This became an overwhelming realization, for it was to be with these artifacts alone that I was committing myself to comprehensively solve all humanity's physio-economic problems.

I then said, "I see the hydrogen atom doesn't have to earn a living before behaving like a hydrogen atom. In fact, as best I can see, only human beings operate on the basis of 'having to earn a living.' The concept is one introduced into social conventions only by the temporal power structure's dictums of the ages. If I am doing what God's evolutionary strategy needs to have accomplished, I need spend no further time worrying about such matters.

"I happen to have been born at the special moment in history in which for the first time there exists enough experience-won and experiment-verified information current in humanity's spontaneous conceptioning and reasoning for all humanity to carry on in a far more intelligent way than ever before.

"I am not being messianically motivated in undertaking this experiment, nor do I think I am someone very special and different from other humans. The design of all humans, like all else in Universe, transcends human comprehension of 'how come' their mysterious, a priori, complexedly designed existence.

"I am doing what I am doing only because at this critical moment I happen to be a human being who, by virtue of a vast number of errors and recognitions of such, has discovered that he would always be a failure as judged by so society's ages-long conditioned reflexings and therefore a 'disgrace' to those related to him (me) in the misassuredly, eternally-to-exist 'not-enough-for-all,' comprehensive, economic struggle of humanity to attain only special, selfish, personal, family, corporate, or national advantage-gaining, wherefore I had decided to commit suicide. I also thereby qualified as a 'throwaway' individual who had acquired enough knowledge regarding relevantly essential human evolution matters to be able to think in this particular kind of way. In committing suicide I seemingly would never again have to feel the pain and mortification of my failures and errors, but the only-by-experience-winnable inventory of knowledge that I had accrued would also be forever lost an inventory of information that, if I did not commit suicide, might prove to be of critical advantage to others, possibly to all others, possibly to Universe." The realization that such a concept could have even a one-in-an-illion chance of being true was a powerful reconsideration provoker and ultimate grand-strategy reorienter.

The thought then came that my impulse to commit suicide was a consequence of my being expressly overconcerned with "me" and "my pains," and that doing so would mean that I would be making the supremely selfish mistake of possibly losing forever some evolutionary information link essential to the ultimate realization of the as-yet-to-be-known human function in Universe. I then realized that I could commit an exclusively ego suicide – a personal-ego "throwaway" – if I swore, to the best of my ability, never again to recognize and yield to the voice of wants only of "me" but instead commit my physical organism and nervous system to enduring whatever pain might lie ahead while possibly thereby coming to mentally comprehend how a "me-less individual might redress the humiliations, expenses, and financial losses I had selfishly and carelessly imposed on all the in-any-way-involved others, while keeping actively alive in toto only the possibly-of-essential-use-for-others inventory of my experience. I saw that there was a true possibility that I could do just that if I remained alive and committed myself to a never-again-for-self-use employment of my omni-experience-gained inventory of knowledge. My thinking began to clear.

I repeated enlargingly to myself, "If I go ahead with my physical suicide, I will selfishly escape from my personal pain but will probably cause great pain to others. I will thereby also throw away the inventory of experience which does not belong to me – that may be of critical evolutionary value to others and even may be said to belong not to me but only to others.

"If I take oath never again to work for my own advantaging and to work only for all others for whom my experience-gained knowledge may be of benefit, I may be justified in not throwing myself away. This will, of course, mean that I will not be able to escape the pain and mortification of being an absolute failure in playing the game of life as it has been taught to me."

I then found myself saying, "I am going to commit myself completely to the wisdom of God and to realization only of the advantages for all humanity potentially existent in what life has already taught and may as yet teach me." I found myself saying, "I am going to commit myself completely to God and to realization of God's apparent intent to assign semi-divine functioning to an as-yet-to-qualify-for-such-functioning humanity. To qualify for such local-Universe's evolutionary adjustings, humans themselves must intelligently discover and spontaneously employ their designed-in potentials and themselves realize the sustainable success of their evolutionarily scheduled physio-economic potential."

From that time, 56 years ago, I have had absolute faith in God. My task was not to preach about God, but to serve God in silence about God. Because such commitment to faith is inherently a "flying blind" commitment, I have often weakened in my confidence in myself to comprehend what it might be that I was being taught or told to do. Because I am a human and designed like all humans to learn only by trial and error, I have had many times to do the wrong things in order thereby to learn what next needed to be done. Making mistakes can be and usually is a very dismaying experience – so dismaying as to make it seemingly easier to "go along with unthinking custom."

If I had not in 1927 committed "egocide," I would probably have yielded long ago to convention and therewith suicide of my "only-for-all-others" initiative.

Friends would say, "You are being treacherous to your wife and child, not going out to earn a living for them. Come over here and we will give you a very good job." When, persuaded by their obvious generosity and concern, I did yield, everything went wrong; and every time I went "off the deep end" again, working only for everybody without salary, everything went right again.

I was convinced from the 1927 outset of this new life that I would be of no benefit whatsoever to the more than two billion humans alive in 1927 if I set about asking people to listen to my ideas and endeavoring to persuade them to reform their thinking and ways of behaving. People listen to you only when in a dilemma they recognize that they don't know what to do and, thinking that you might know, ask you to advise them what to do. When they do ask you and you have only a seemingly "good idea" of what they might do, you are far less effective than when you can say "Jump aboard and I'll take you where you want to go" or "Jump aboard that vehicle and it will take you to where you want to go." This involves an inanimate artifact to "jump aboard."

Quite clearly I had to address not only the specific but also the comprehensive problem of how to find ways of giving human beings more energy-effective environment-controlling artifacts that did ever more environment-controlling with ever less pounds of materials, ergs of energy, and minutes of time per each realized functioning, until we attained the physically realized techno-energetic ability to do so much with so little that we could realize ample good-life support for everyone, hoping that under those more favorable physical circumstances humans would dare to be less selfish and more genuinely thoughtful toward one another, instead of being lethally and subversively competitive for a share in the existing misassumed-to-be-fundamental inadequacy of life support, perpetually to be extant, on our planet. Every time I recommitted myself so to do, everything went well again.

So we – my wife and family – have for 56 years realized a series of miracles that occur just when I need something, but not until the absolutely last second. If what I think I need does not become available I realize that my objective may be invalid or that I am steering a wrong course. It is only through such nonhappenings that I seem to be informed of how to correct both my grand strategy and its constituent initiations.

I can't make plans of how to invest that which I don't have or don't know that I am going to have. I cannot count on anything. During all these last 56 years I have been unable to budget. I simply have to have faith and just when I need the right-something for the right-reasoning, there it is – or there they are – the workshops, helping hands, materials, ideas, money, tools.

Throughout the last 56 years, I have been able to initiate and manage a great many physical-artifact developments, well over $20 million direct-expenditures' worth of artifact-prototype-producing-and-testing physical research and development. For the last twenty years my income has averaged a quarter of a million dollars a year and my office overhead, travel, invention research and development, and taxes have also averaged a quarter of a million dollars. I am always operating in proximity to bankruptcy but never going bankrupt. While I owe all the humans of all history an unrepayable debt of only-by-experience-winnable knowledge, I don't owe anybody any money and have never consciously and deliberately gained at the expense of others.

I have no accrued savings of earnings. Income taxes take away even the most meager cushioning of funds. I have no retirement fund. I am on nobody's retirement roll. My wife's and my own social security combine to $9,000 per year. The tax experts tell me that the base of the U.S. government taxing theory relates to capitalism and its initially-amassed-dollars-investments in physical production facilities and the progressive depreciation of those physical properties. I operate in a differently accounted world in which there is nothing that I can depreciate wherewith to accrue further-initiative-funding capability. The "know-how" capital capability with which I operate is always appreciating at an exponentially multiplying rate.

There is always an inventory of important follow-through tasks to be accomplished and a number of new, highly relevant critical initiatives to be taken.

Over the years there have also had to be a number of important errors to be made and important lessons to be learned. From the outset of my 1927 commitment and the first twenty subsequent years, there were individuals who were altruistically inspired to support my commitment. For instance, in 1928 a lawyer friend of mine gave me his services for nothing. Seeing the advantage for me of incorporating my activity, he took a few shares in my corporation to pay for his very prodigious services with a hope of incidental personal profit (see my book 4 D Timelock). Fortunately, the individual investments of those who sought to help me were as monetarily small as they were altruistically large, for their direct profits were never realized and their investments seemingly lost, unless they felt greatly rewarded, as many did, to discover that they had helped to launch an enterprise that as years went on seemed to be ever more promising for all humanity.

The last such "ultimately lost," friendly financial backing occurred during my design and production of the Dymaxion Dwelling Machine's mass-production prototype for Beech Aircraft in Wichita, Kansas. It was there, in 1944, 1945, and 1946, that I produced in full working scale the Dymaxion House, which weighed the three tons that I had estimated and published it would weigh when I designed it in 1927-29. This Beech-Dymaxion realized weight of three tons proved the validity of both my structural and economic efficacious theory and its important technological advance over its conventional, equi-volumed and - equipped counterpart residence of 1927, which weighed 150 tons. It was the 1927 design-initiative discovery that I could apparently by physical design reduce fifty-fold the weight of materials necessary to produce a home, given certain operating standards, that gave me a "rocket blast-off" as an increase of confidence in my theory of solving humans' economic problems by producing ever more performance with ever less energy investments. The confirmation realized at Beech Aircraft seventeen years later was a second-stage rocket acceleration of my only-by-artifact problem-solving initiative.

Produced on the premises of Beech Aircraft, this 1944 mass-production dwelling machine prototype was ordered and paid for by the U.S. Air Force. The prototype, along with its 100 percent spare parts, cost $54,000 and after World War II was turned over by the government to a privately organized two-hundred-thousand-dollar corporation formed by about 300 subscribers – averaging a $666 gamble. This corporation hoped to organize the mass production of the physically realized and three-times-refined government-paid-for prototype. Beech Aircraft had its production engineering department plan the tooling and complete an estimate of producing the Dymaxion Dwelling Machine at a rate of 20,000 per year. Beech then made a firm offer to produce them at that rate for $1,800 each, delivered in Wichita minus the kitchen equipment and other electrical appliances to be provided by General Electric on a rental basis of $200 a year. Beech required, however, that a ten-million-dollar tooling cost be provided by outside finance. This was not raised because there existed no high-speed, one-day, "turnkey" – no marketing, distributing, and installing service industry. Prepayment checks for 37,000 unsolicited orders had to be returned. The hopefully-into-mass-production gamble of the private corporation occurred despite my two-fold warning that (1) experience had by then taught me that the gains accruing to my work apparently were distributable only to everybody and only as techno-economic advantage profits for all humanity and (2) that while I was producing an important prototype dwelling machine suitable for mass production at a low cost, there existed as yet no distribution and maintenance service industry (and that the latter would require a development period taking another third of a century).

No one has ever won their direct monetary gains by their investment-for-profit bets on my artifact-inventing and - developing concepts. I have always been saddened by this because the backers' motives were most often greatly affected by a personal affection for me. Fortunately, this gambling on the financial success of my work despite my warnings seems altogether to have ceased a third of a century ago.

With several hundred thousand geodesic domes, millions of my world maps and books, and structural and mechanical artifacts now distributed and installed around the world, I have realized new and ever greater degrees of technical advantaging of society and its individuals. I have continually increased the knowledge of the means of accomplishing across-the-board and world-around advances in technological abilities to produce more economically effective structures and machinery that do ever more work with ever less pounds of materials, ergs of energy, and seconds of time per function – all accomplished entirely within the visible structural inventions and invisible (alloying, electronic, etc.) realms of technology. Twelve years ago I had learned enough to be able to state publicly that humanity had now passed through an evolutionary inflection point whereafter, for the first time in history, it is irrefutably demonstrable that a ten-year design revolution that employs all the physical resources of humanity (now majorly invested in killingry technology) and transforms weaponry scrap into livingry technology, can, within ten design-science-revolution years, have all humanity enjoying a higher standard of living – interminably sustainable – than any humans have ever experienced, while concurrently phasing out all further everyday uses of fossil fuels or atomic energy. We can live handsomely using only our daily income of the Sun's and gravity's multi-way-intergenerated energies.

This omni-humanity eco-technical breakthrough opportunity involves the successful inauguration of the industrial mass production of the dwelling machines and all other geodesic and tensegrity, air-deliverable, move-in-today, environmental controls. The technology for producing the dwelling machines, their air deliverability, their energy harvesting and conserving, and their prolonged autonomy of operation, has now reached the service industry launching stage. The dwelling machine service industry will not sell houses but will only rent them (as with rental cars or telephones). Much of the dead U.S. automobile-manufacturing industry can and probably will be retooled to produce the dwelling machines that will be needed to upgrade the deployed phases of living of four billion humans. The environment-controlling service industry will provide city-size domes for protecting and housing humanity's convergent activities and the dwelling machine will accommodate all humanity's divergent activities.

My part in this half-century-long technological development has all been fulfilled or occurred as an absolute miracle. From what I have learned I can say – at this most critical moment in all the history of humanity – that whether we are going to stay here or not depends entirely on each and all of our individually attained and maintained integrities of reasoning and acting and not on any politically or religiously accepted or power-imposed socioeconomic-credo-system or financial reforms.

At the outset of my 1927 commitment to exploring for that which only the individual could do effectively for all humanity, while depending entirely on the unpromised-to-him backing of his enterprise only by God, it became immediately evident that if indeed the undertaking became affirmatively supported by God, it would entail many extraordinary physical and metaphysical insights regarding both human and cosmic affairs. I asked myself, "(1) Can you trust yourself never to turn to your own exclusive advantage the insights entrusted to you only for the realization of benefits for all humanity and Universe itself? (2) Can you also be sure that you will never exploit your insight by publicly declaring yourself to be a special 'son of God' or a divinely ordained mystic leader? (3) Can you trust yourself to remember that you qualified for this functioning only because you were an out-and-out throwaway? (4) Can you trust yourself to reliably report these facts to others when they applaud you for the success of the experiment with which you were entrusted?"

Fortunately, I can, may, and do report to you that I have never broken that trust nor have I ever been tempted to do so.

I do not deem it to be a breaking of that trust when – entirely unsolicited by me or by my family or by any of those working with me on my staff – individuals or organizations outside my domain come spontaneously to me or my staff to employ me as a speaker, author, architect, or consultant. It is these unsolicited, uncontrived, spontaneous short-engagement employments of me in one role or another, plus – on rare occasions – an unsolicited outright gift to me of money, materials, tools, working space, commissions for designs, orders for specific products, etc., which altogether uncontrived employments and unsought gifts I have classified for you as the "miracles," always unforeseeable-in-advance, which have financed or implemented my technical initiatives.

I hope this book will prove to be an encouraging example of what the little, average human being can do if you have absolute faith in the eternal cosmic intelligence we call God.

# PATENTS

"I said, 'How do we find out how to use our minds and experience to the highest advantage of others in the shortest possible time?' That was the challenge. Out of this, in due course, came a great many designs, because I said to myself, 'I must commit myself to reforming the environment and not man; being absolutely confident that if you give man the right environment he will behave favorably.'"

*~Quoted from Buckminster Fuller An Autobiographical Monologue/Scenario, by Robert Snyder, page 39*

The following patents were the results of this commitment of Bucky's:

1. Stockade: Building Structure (1927)      U.S. Patent 1,633,702

2. Stockade: Pneumatic Forming Process (1927)  U.S. Patent 1,634,900

3. 4D House (1928) Application abandoned by Buckminster Fuller, leaving prior art evidence in patent office files.

4. Dymaxion Car (1937)      U.S. Patent 2,101,057

5. Dymaxion Bathroom (1940)      U.S. Patent 2,220,482

6. Dymaxion Deployment Unit (sheet) (1944)  U.S. Patent 2,343,764

7. Dymaxion Deployment Unit (frame) (1944)  U.S. Patent 2,351,419

8. Dymaxion Map (1946)      U.S. Patent 2,393,676

9. Dymaxion House (Wichita) (1946)

10. Geodesic Dome (1954)      U.S. Patent 2,682,235

11. Paperboard Dome (1959)      U.S. Patent 2,881,717

12. Plydome (1959)      U.S. Patent 2,905,113

13. Catenary (Geodesic Tent) (1959)      U.S. Patent 2,914,074

14. Octet Truss (1961)      U.S. Patent 2,986,241

15. Tensegrity (1962)      U.S. Patent 3,063,521

16. Submarisle (Undersea Island) (1963)  U.S. Patent 3,080,583

17. Aspension (Suspension Building) (1964)    U.S. Patent 3,139,957

18. Monohex (Geodesic Structures) (1965)    U.S. Patent 3,197,927

19. Laminar Dome (1965)    U.S. Patent 3,203,144

20. Octa Spinner (1965) Application abandoned by Buckminster Fuller, leaving prior art evidence in patent office files.

21. Star Tensegrity (Octahedral Truss) (1967)    U.S. Patent 3,354,591

22. Rowing Needles (Watercraft) (1970)    U.S. Patent 3,524,422

23. Geodesic Hexa-pent (1974)    U.S. Patent 3,810,336

24. Floatable Breakwater (1975)    U.S. Patent 3,863,455

25. Non-symmetrical Tensegrity (1975)    U.S. Patent 3,866,366

26. Floating Breakwater (1979)    U.S. Patent 4,136,994

27. Tensegrity Truss (1980)    U.S. Patent 4,207,715

28. Hanging Storage Self Unit (1983)    U.S. Patent 4,377,114

# HONORARY DOCTORATE CITATIONS

1.  *Design,* North Carolina Sate College of Agriculture and Engineering; Raleigh, North Carolina (1954)

2.  *Arts,* University of Michigan; Ann Arbor, Michigan (1955)

3.  *Science,* Washington University; St. Louis, Missouri (1657)

4.  *Arts,* Southern Illinois University; Carbondale, Illinois (1959)

5.  *Humane Letters,* Rollins College; Winter Park, Florida (1960)

6.  *Letters,* Clemson College; Clemson, South Carolina (1964)

7.  *Fine Arts,* University of New Mexico; Albuquerque, New Mexico (1964)

8.  *Science,* University of Colorado; Boulder, Colorado (1964)

9.  *Humane Letters,* Monmouth College; Monmouth, Illinois (1964)

10. *Humane Letters,* Long Island University, Zeckendorf Campus; Brooklyn, New York (1966)

11. *Humane Letters,* San Jose State College; San Jose, California (1966)

12. *Fine Arts,* California College of Arts and Crafts; Oakland, California (1966)

13. *Engineering,* Clarkson College of Technology; Postdam, New York (1967)

14. *Fine Arts,* Ripon College; Ripon, Wisconsin (1968)

15. *Humane Letters,* Dartmouth College; Hanover, New Hampshire (1968)

16. *Humane Letters,* New England College; Henniker, New Hampshire (1968)

17. *Humane Letters,* University of Rhode Island; Kinston, Rhode Island (1968)

18. *Architectural Engineering,* University of Wisconsin; Milwaukee, Wisconsin (1969)

19. *Fine Arts,* Boston College; Boston, Massachusetts (1969)

20. *Science,* Bates College; Lewiston, Maine (1969)

21. *Fine Arts,* College of Art and Design; Minneapolis, Minnesota (1970)

22. *Laws,* Park College; Parkville, Missouri (1970)

23. *Humane Letters,* Brandeis University; Waltham, Massachusetts (1970)

24. *Humane Letters,* Columbia College; Chicago, Illinois (1970)

25. *Science and Humane Letters*, Wilberforce University; Wilberforce, Ohio (1970)

26. *Fine and Applied Arts*, Southeastern Massachusetts University; North Dartmouth, Massachusetts (1971)

27. *Laws*, Grinell College; Grinnell, Iowa (1972)

28. *Laws*, Emerson College; Boston, Massachusetts (1972)

29. *Science*, University of Maine; Orono, Maine (1972)

30. *Laws*, Nasson College; Springvale, Maine (1973)

31. *Fine Arts*, Rensselaer Polytechnic Institute; Troy, New York (1973)

32. *Literature*, Beaver College; Glenside, Pennsylvania (1973)

33. *Engineering*, University of Notre Dame, Notre Dame, Indiana (1974)

34. *Humane Letters*, Saint Joseph's College; Philadelphia, Pennsylvania

35. *Science*, Pratt Institute; Brooklyn, New York (1974)

36. *Science*, McGill University; Montreal, Quebec, Canada (1974)

37. *Humane Letters*, Hobart and William Smith Colleges of the Seneca; Geneva, New York (1975)

38. *Science*, Hahnemann Medical College & Hospital of Pennsylvania, Philadelphia, Pennsylvania (1978)

39. *Humane Letters*, Southern Ilinois University; Edwardsville, Illinois (1979)

40. *Humane Letters*, Alaska Pacific University; Anchorage, Alaska (1979)

41. *Humane Letters*, Roosevelt University; Chicago, Illinois (1980)

42. *Humanities*, Georgian Court College; Lakewood, New Jersey (1980)

# BOOKS BY R. BUCKMINSTER FULLER

1. 4D Timelock, 1928
2. Nine Chains to the Moon, 1938
3. The Dymaxion World of Buckminster Fuller, 1960
4. Education Automation, 1962
5. Untitled Epic Poem on the History of Industrialization, 1962
6. Ideas and Integrities, 1963
7. No More Second Hand God, 1963
8. R. Buckminster Fuller on Education, 1963
9. World Design Science Decade Documents, 1965-1975
10. What I Have Learned "How Little I Know", 1968
11. Utopia or Oblivion 1969
12. Operating Manual for Spaceship Earth, 1969
13. The Buckminster Fuller Reader, 1970
14. Buckminster Fuller to Children of Earth, 1972
15. Intuition, 1972
16. Earth, Inc., 1973
17. Tetrascroll: Goldilocks and the Three Bears, 1975
18. Synergetics: Explorations in the Geometry of Thinking, 1975
19. And It Came to Pass - Not to Stay, 1976
20. Synergetics Folio, 1979
21. Synergetics 2: Further Explorations in the Geometry of Thinking, 1979
22. Buckminster Fuller Sketchbook, 1980
23. Critical Path, 1981
24. Grunch of Giants, 1983
25. Inventions: The Patented Works of R. Buckminster Fuller, 1983
26. Humans in Universe (with Anwar Dil), 1983
27. The Artifacts of R. Buckminster Fuller, 1984
28. Cosmography, 1992